SUN RISING INTO STORM

SUN RISING INTO STORM

poems

James Bertolino

MoonPath Press

Copyright © 2021 James Bertolino

All rights reserved. No part of this publication may be reproduced, distributed, or transmitted in any form or by any means whatsoever without written permission from the publisher, except in the case of brief excerpts for critical reviews and articles. All inquiries should be addressed to MoonPath Press.

Poetry
ISBN 978-1-936657-59-9

Cover photo by Anita K. Boyle of a detail of her collage *Unearthing Semantics*, 2021

Author photo by Anita K. Boyle

Book design by Tonya Namura, using Gentium Basic

MoonPath Press, an imprint of Concrete Wolf Poetry Series, is dedicated to publishing the finest poets living in the U.S. Pacific Northwest.

MoonPath Press
PO Box 445
Tillamook, OR 97141

MoonPathPress@gmail.com

http://MoonPathPress.com

for Anita

Acknowledgments

Poems in this collection have had prior publication by *Adventures NW*, Cave Moon Press, *Cirque*, *Chrysanthemum*, *Clover*, *Five Willows Review*, *Lit Fuse*, Other Mind Press, *Poet Lore*, Quarterly Review of Literature Award Series, *Raven Chronicles*, *Rosebud*, Rose Alley Press, *Snail River*, *Van Gogh's Ear Anthology*, University of Washington Press, and *Washington 129*.

Contents

Ten-Foot Gnarly Stick	3
Timing	4
Vision Willed	5
Which Species?	6
White Tails	7
Tissue	8
Shiver	9
The Wave	10
The Oregon Shore	11
Traveling Face-Down	12
In the Woods with Jericho	13
Appropriate Behavior	14
Another Holiday at Risk	15
Another Dead Refrigerator Poem	16
St. Irwin, the Martyr	17
Pacific Prayer	18
Whales	19
The Woman Who Collaborates	20
Spiked Snake	21
Angel	22
Amputee	23
Compost	24
Elephants	25
Housing	26
See Willow: A Pantoum	27
Twisted Warrior	28
Like Taut Persimmon	29
A Tone Becomes	30
The Mending	31
The Flying Dwarf	32
Near McCracken's Pond	33
The Adequacy	34
The Return	35
A Spring Crocus: For Those Who Briefly Live	36
The Reach That Exceeds	37

Uroboros	38
Beach Stones	39
The Symbols	40
A Song for M.	41
Starbumps	42
Snow Goose	43
The Stripper	44
The Swallow	45
Virus Charisma: A Mutant Pantoum	46
Her Name Was Roca	47
The Better Path: A Pantoum	48
Sequoia	49
Shiva Takes Hold	50
Mounted	51
The Woman	52
Ghost	53
Ecstasy	54
The Slide	55
The System	56
Frost	57
Swimming Lesson	58
Naming	61
Around the Bend	62
Lookout Creek	63
The Salamander	64
Pondering	65
Winter Spiders	66
Winter Sapling	67
Ode to No Snow	68
Winter Nocturne	69
Saved by Moss	70
Toothpicks	71
White Boulders	72
Endless	73
About the Author	75

SUN RISING INTO STORM

Ten-Foot Gnarly Stick

I found this great stick on one of my brief
hikes in Oregon's Andrews Forest.
Its length is slightly arced, and it has
rich character. I comprehend and treasure it
as the arc of my life. My seventy years begin
at the blunt end, and it runs pretty straight
for about three feet. Then things get very interesting:
there are sudden curves, and protruding knobs,
and it never marks a straight line for more than
a few inches at a time. There are gouges,
dark spots, and places where it threatens
to split. But there is a steady progression until
about nine inches from the end, where it makes
a sharp, left-hand turn. What, I wonder,
can that mean?

Timing

1.
Too late to find
the large man
who juggles canaries.

2.
Quite taken by the roses
so beautifully
brutalized this late
in their season.

3.
Never to know
the comradeship
of smokers.

4.
In this society
if ever you are to be
accepted, you must bind
your wings.

5.
Could you listen
carefully enough
to a stone, you would hear
the pulsing atoms murmur
"birth...birth...birth."

Vision Willed

Once we submerge
the only way to survive
is to breathe the sea.

Swedenborg said angels
are 216 feet tall,
and he was a knowledgeable man.

A moth's wing dust sifts
down the mirror
defining the invisible.

In the middle of a common event,
like all creatures of intelligence,
we come to will how we see.

Which Species?

Our species has developed
a new relationship with this planet,
one where we insist on inflicting damage.
While we have contributed grandly
to global warming, like sniveling brats
we complain of being punished for something
we insist we have not done. Sounds like a relationship
gone wrong. I'm wondering what the Pope thinks
about the obvious sinful behaviors.

White Tails

Certain poems, usually short ones,
have little white tails—like bunny rabbits.
They typically lead the way.

But don't expect a bunny-poem
to come when you call. You need
to be ready to greet them

whenever they arrive.
Consider yourself honored
when a bunny poem has chosen you!

Tissue

The scant glow
of firefly

smeared between a child's
thumb and finger:

its visible soul
diminishes

as her hand reaches back
to the steady dark.

Shiver

She stood there shivering
and dampened by the rain.
Facing the forest, which was a blaze

of autumn color, she was unaware
of the bones beneath the trees.
But so much of what she'd long believed

was now twisted, her heart broken.
Life is like that. We witness vitality,
yet know that it is passing,

and all too soon we learn
to accept our own end
being near.

The Wave

Once again we learn order
watching the legs

of the centipede: such
elegance—to make

the precise move,
to know when, and be

convinced your motion
is of the great wave of being.

The Oregon Shore

We found her bound
to a heavily buried
lodgepole pine,

where her appearance
resembled a snarling mastiff.
It was somewhat frightening,

and we caught ourselves
making what sounded like moans.
I was embarrassed,

and my companion kept looking
away. But while for us it felt
like the end had come,

we did get home alive.

Traveling Face-Down

Traveling face-down, no sentient machine
can know his weakness, nothing suspects

that behind his corpulence there is history
both dangerous and benign. His path

has taken a fork in the flesh, where death
and life are braided like husband and wife.

There is a grieving in the cells, which opens him
to being eaten by the great black mouth between

the stars. His weary eyes find poisoned humus—
now bereft of earthworm, beetle and fungus.

He remembers all that had leaped
and crawled, that oozed and groped toward

a future Nature ruled.
Now evil resides in the molecules.

Now life is a fabric of circuit
and tortured light.

In the Woods with Jericho

A beer in the woods,
accompanied by Jericho Brown
in the form of his 2019
Copper Canyon Press volume
titled *The Tradition*.

Jericho and I are are related
in both being Copper Canyon Press poets,
though my volume, *Making Space For
Our Living*, goes back a ways to 1975.

Here's a quote from Brown:

"If I needed anyone to look at me,
I'd dye my hair purple
and live in Bemidji."

I've been to Bemidji, and comprehend
his perspective.

Imagine a handsome black man
with purple hair!

Were he hitch-hiking, I would stop and
invite him in.

Appropriate Behavior

When a frog is tiny enough
to hide in a thimble, let it be.

When a snake is moving
in elegant curves through the grass,
watch your step.

If your neighbor smiles
around a long carrot
protruding from his mouth,

you might say "It's obvious
you'd rather smoke a vegetable
than a cigar!"

There are numerous ways
to honor the world.

Another Holiday at Risk

In love early, and already
in pain. Every several steps

a bad one, building by slips a structure
of discomfort. Is he a scrawny

Christmas tree hung with apologies?
Will he never be clear? Why each gesture

smeared with self-doubt, emotion sawed
and severed? She so dear and new

in her loving, he one falter after the next, one strain.
He prays that he not destroy the frail

ecstasy visited on him like clustered
wine, like grapes of light.

Another Dead Refrigerator Poem

I give you a board walking
and you ask for more:
not enough wiggly stuff,
hardly a keeper.

Well, the bug is back, stylish
high-stepping
adventure-boy. I guess
he knows where he's loved.

Likes cotton sweaters,
burlap too, but get him back
on a blue-lined yellow pad
and you'll see him strut, stretch

like the world's his cookie.
So I turn on the microphone,
and say "okay, blenny-girl,
start crooning!"

St. Irwin, the Martyr

Sorcerer, mutant, call him
what you will. He spoke of bird
funnels, and of the breathing mountains
before America drowned.
He described Earth's magnetic shells
as loose sheets of being, but the Pentagon
shot him down.

Memory is the backside of appetite
he taught us, we ingest the universe
with our forgetfulness. He said the door
to the world of surfaces swings in and
swings out with breath. It opens with breathing
and closes with our deaths.

Our bodies pay homage to the forms.

He wrote of sex as a ladder only two can climb.
His torturers remembered this
when they found him. In the chapel
to Nikola Tesla, which he built of steady orbits
at the age of twenty-three, they suspended
him on seven lasers like a nude quail
sizzling on a spit.

They jeered, "Wink out, you fool!"

But he was afraid, and fear is the black chute,
the nanosecond that never ends.
So he converted the pain, and rode it out.

Pacific Prayer

As the Spring rhody
unfolds it dewy mauve

and the frogs spread
the webbed song

they have come to give,
we put our palms together

and thank Heaven
we are alive.

Whales

In the mountain's
white expanse

beyond the tree line,
we learned

Buddhist holy men
come again as humpback whales:

the greater their mastery,
the further back in time.

The Woman Who Collaborates

There is a woman who collaborates
with the sun. She is water,
she's fire. She makes the melon ripen
and the squash blossoms flower.

There is a woman who celebrates
with the tides—every mollusk
wakens to her name. Every kelp string
and weed swims to her breathing.

There is a woman who collaborates with air,
who brings the ancient forests to flame.
She laughs and mountains explode.
She hums and the earth shudders open.

There is a woman who collaborates
with our dream. Our long fears love her,
and she is our leader, she is to blame.

Spiked Snake

Not what you seem,
never the image
others see,

nor how you
appear when you study
the mirror.

Your smile quivers
over teeth gone feral.

Then the hot
spiked snake climbs
the curve
of your spine,

and you burn, your face
a glaze of pain.

Angel

Being visited
by an angel

(invisible, subtle)
is like every cell

in your body being
kissed by

this world's
softest lips.

Amputee

It was all she knew
of the amputee issue.

"The bliss is untenable,"
she said, and spoke of a "swarm
that complicates the tongue.

Avoid stray marks and corner rust.
Revive the hunger for cost."
We learned then our one decision

is made by grief-light,
and as we toasted the new
gangrene paste procedure,

her face became an open wound.

Compost

When a deer
severs

the green shoots
and leaves

then poops soft pebbles,
it is not death

but composted life
it has left.

Elephants

Near the center of the Book Festival,
creating an island of turbulence

in the nervous herd, and sounding
like two elephant cows

crooning to the little ones, were huddled
the wheelchair poets, palsied of body

and speech, but of love, strong,
of love, clear.

Housing

The opportunistic
ground spider,

like his distant cousin
the hermit crab,

enlists the empty
gopher hole

as the perfect nose
for his funnel of web.

See Willow: A Pantoum

At last you'll know why you came.
See willow. Feel willow.
Hold to the proof of loons.
This day is like no other.

See willow. Feel willow.
Feel the slender spirit of the reeds.
This day is like no other.
Step wisely along the stones.

Feel the slender spirit of the reeds.
There are crows discussing the moon.
Step wisely along the stones.
The blue jay says believe.

There are crows discussing the moon.
Feel wind inside the cedar.
The blue jay says believe.
A star descends and everything rises.

Feel wind inside the cedar.
Hold to the proof of loons.
A star descends and everything rises.
At last you know why you came.

Twisted Warrior

Hungry for the big defeat,
he harried the strong ones,

then teased the tight-faced scuttlers
till they could take no more.

He dreamed of challenge, the abyss
as measure of the man.

But when he spoke of the final test,
he lied. In the end,

what he sought
was simply death.

Like Taut Persimmon

Come, lie down
where your hair may yearn
into the earth, where fear
is the last garment you fling.

Columbine and rain, azalea
and sunrise,
the world reaches
with two hands, two wings
over the hills.

Rest for a feathered moment
over the depths, then ease
your long-limbed spirit beyond
limitation. Stand naked
in the river of arrival.

Now wave to someone you love.

Like ripe pear, like taut
persimmon,
you fill with
mystical sugars.

A Tone Becomes

Again it's that time
when she needs to make

something beautiful,
as a poet might do.

To shape a gathering,
where a sound might repeat,

where a tone becomes
a trough in the pattern,

in the wave. After so long
a time to simply say

something true:
Her planet has moved.

The Mending

His one desire: to suffer
the tearing that mends,

to die into the new order
one last time.

Everything is starting
and finished.

The raven has spoken
his new name.

The Flying Dwarf

Today I remember my life
as a dwarf, hands like
flattened kidneys,
fingers fat brown pickles,
only shorter—I still move my hands
as clumsily as then.

There was a brooding to all
I did or felt, a heaviness.
My stubbed legs kept me close
to the earth, where the dead and
decaying find ease. Though stunted,
I was impervious to disease.

The only living thing I ever loved
was a chicken, and it died
before I was through. When nearly
finished with that life, I knew
there would be another, where my fate would
resemble an alchemical model called
"the limitation of four."

If finally I flew, it would be without
a body, or on wings
of sufficient enormity to bear
the full burden of my species.

Near McCracken's Pond

Got so still
the frog

remembered
its tail

and a bird
gazed through

the eyes of
a dinosaur.

The Adequacy

To father, who asked,
I say we've gathered these years
to learn the adequacy
of caprice.

Our lives follow the goat

and this vitality is as much of horror
as we deserve.

We will be responsible.
Where there is beauty
there is not defeat.

Between tribe and estrangement
we sink into the grasses
with the horses feeding
and brushing the flies away.

We hold for some moments
what will never change.

The Return

Each breath
that you release
gives to the world a trace
of your thoughts

and feelings.
This in return
for the inspiration
the world gives you.

A Spring Crocus:
For Those Who Briefly Live

There are children
who diminish
as they grow,

who will never be grown,
or be parents,
or be old.

Their few days smolder
like the sun rising
into a storm.

And those who love
hold them precious
and brave

as the first Spring crocus,
whose small yellow blaze
might brighten

a morning still held dim
by Winter. Such
blossoming

refutes the cold.

The Reach That Exceeds

Reaching
for the comfort
of definition

you touch
darkness.

Uroboros

Following the sound
of a waterfall down

through the redwoods
to a stone bowl

where stream gathers
before leaping:

spinning there is the roil
like a snake with tail in its mouth—

its curved dimensions, green above,
orange below, become a twisting

Mobius strip: a wedding ring
binding eternity with time.

Beach Stones

Pain several parts pleasure,
with tender bare feet
he crossed the beach stones
remembering the thousands

of people he had stepped on
and over in his career—some few
dented or damaged him,
but most had been a massage

for the musculature
of his ambition.
                        Suddenly a large
shore crab drew blood
from his curled pink toe.

Standing on one leg, weaving,
his violated foot held in both hands,
he knew that soon his dominion
would end.

The Symbols

Do you remember when a chorus
of fat moon frogs
terrified what lurks below
the Safeway store?

Now each Winter night a throng
of red ghosts stalk
the lone violinist who plays Gershwin
while walking home from the bowling alley.

He visualizes bone-sized glimmers of the future.

In the apartment, someone new
is standing on her head
in an oil painting strewn
with salsa and guacamole.

Time to begin counting the signs:
there is a manic hen in
the port-a-potty, and on a warehouse
wall there are symbols for suicide
and interplanetary miscegenation.

A Song for M.

We are not equal.

There are souls created close
to the greatness:

Life-to-life they are
more often confined
than not.

Somehow the spirit grows.

One of those was Marilyn
Monroe.

Starbumps

In the stark middle
of the night

he's outside standing naked
on the back deck of his house,

shivering. His hands move over
his arms and chest, while he gazes deep

into the dazzling stellar field.
A breeze has raised goose bumps

by the thousands, and now each
is connected to one of the stars.

The chill becomes pleasure
as his body says "hello"

to the universe.

Snow Goose

It was 3 a.m. I felt
my dream chute rip
and tumbled free, bare knees
and elbows
flippant in starlight.

It was funny, spiraling
down the chilled miles
like a snow goose crippled
by love. I say, you

there, listening behind transparent
feathers of caution, remember
when being cool meant being
copacetic? Do you recall
the metaphysics of rope?

Yes, it was grotesque then, long
before the grand shimmer,
the return of Her Yellowness,
Lord Bile.

The Stripper

His younger sister, who always
had an interest in the details

of her own body, had now risen
without remorse from the wetland of memory.

She makes her living as a stripper,
doing her lovely grind in public,

and the tavern begins to shake.
It's the earthquake she works into her act,

and the patrons know it's time to run
for cover, or prepare to die.

The Swallow

Floating downstream, she felt sunlight
become liquid, felt it reaching
into her ears, her lips.
No longer her being carried by the stream,
she was the stream, and the sun's photons
were tiny explosions of feeling.

She became aware of deep vibration
and of moving more rapidly: her liquid body
shot over the lip of a waterfall and off
into space. She broke into thousands of droplets,
each a point of ecstasy. She was a sigh of pleasure
as she spread into mist. Then a swallow

flew through her. She knew
a loving the universe finds in the swallow's
existence, the way its sensual form
becomes intimate with damp air.

She felt water
on her wings.

Virus Charisma: A Mutant Pantoum

"Kiss me," she said, "without your mouth."
He wrote her name in pink petals
across the floor of his cell.
She touched him with her virus charisma

on the planet where desire always leads to death.
He wrote her name in pink across his room.
"Feigning indifference," she said, "proves your love
on this planet where desire leads to death."

His lips against her tasted promises un-kept.
Such displays of indifference, he thought,
would cause riots in any city.
While his lips brushed her neck,

she complained his weepy spill
could bring wilderness into the city.
He wondered if love had become a sickness,
proven by his weakened spill.

He knew then why women cheated their wombs—
they had been touched by virus charisma.
Her fingers shaped a missing fetus. "Kiss him,"
she whispered, "without your mouth."

Her Name Was Roca

Once again my heart
gutted by a cat,

she a catalog of loved gestures,
of life-shaped sounds.

How tell the thrill
of fingers electric with
the epiphany of her fur?

That subtle epistemology: fur
softer than identity.

My head gone now
with her pink nose,
her high cirrus eyes.

Some loss,
some lamb.

The Better Path: A Pantoum

I killed my friend today.
I thought it the better path,
though if death was what he wanted,
he didn't say. He hurt a lot, yet grinned.

I thought it was the better path.
He always met my eyes with love, and when
he said he hurt a lot, he grinned.
I killed my friend this afternoon

because he met my eyes with love.
We knew it was time, so I killed
my love this afternoon.
He fought a little, only a little,

because he knew it was time.
At the end I had some help.
He fought a little, but we knew
it was right to do.

At the end I needed help,
though death was what he wanted.
He knew it was right to do.
Today I killed my friend.

Sequoia

When fire moves
like a flood and

each smallest breath
is a claim, each sigh

a relinquishing, you ask
what a thousand-year-old Sequoia

has learned of the wind.
What does it desire?

When only the tallest prayers
rise beyond black clouds

blistering the sky, it's time
to embrace what burns.

Spirit confirms what matter knows.

Shiva Takes Hold

Like need shivering
on the brink
of knowledge,
she lifts her ear
toward Andromeda,
while all around the singing
of pond peepers and crickets,
the shrill piping of the velvet-winged
find form

in her mind.
Silky goddess, intimate
of the rapture that begins
with moss licking feet and ends
in the stars: Shiva takes hold

by her hair
and pulls her through
to the other world.

Mounted

Riding east,
my fingers

travel through
the horse's

mane.

The Woman

Her thoughts
clothe
the distance
my whisper climbs
through the dark:

This shape is old
and fetal.

Ghost

The ghost
that has been haunting
your bedroom
for weeks
finally speaks:

"All I want
is a cup of coffee."

Ecstasy

God touched
her ear
with a butterly
wing,

while the devil
pushed mud up
between
her toes.

The Slide

They passed a stand
of lover's lichen,
and were reminded
of the blue slide,

the slow parabola
a thought describes
when the pain of dying
exhausts itself,

and a noise like water
crossing porcelain
becomes a climate
which supports its own

marvelous profusion
of living forms.

The System

The more grand
what you desire is,
the more it is desire
that sustains you.

On the way to eternity,
it's the days.

Frost

An early frost has gathered
on the underside of leaves.

A breeze over the pond
has sharpened, and petals fall.

The rust- and black-banded
caterpillar shudders with ruin.

Swimming Lesson

I was shooting baskets
with a neighbor girl—we were both 16.
Though just a tomboy friend, and not
someone I considered a relationship,
I did enjoy watching her breasts
when she made jump-shots. It was Summer
and she wore a halter top.

A car drove up, a '53 Dodge convertible,
with two guys, neither of whom I recognized.
They honked. She passed the ball to me
and skipped out to the street. At one point,
she gestured in my direction,
and the guys looked angry, or glum.
They laid rubber when they drove off.

She strutted back with a grin and made
a pass toward the basket. I slipped the ball
to her and she went in for an easy lay-up.
She told me she was going with those guys to Izaack Walton
that afternoon, to go swimming. My instincts
said "no," but thinking of the beer, I said, "sure."

They picked me up at my house. The driver,
an older guy who must have bought the beer,
had a girl with him in the front seat.
She wasn't good-looking, and a little overweight.
Everybody talked about class in those days,
and they seemed pretty low—maybe farmers,
or from the West Side. He was big, and quiet.
The other guy, in the back with my neighbor, was smaller
than me, and scruffy. I climbed in with them.

As it turned out, only my pal and I had swimming suits.
The others were interested in drinking and munching chips.
It was like a picnic. So she and I went down through the
    woods
to the river, where we rough-housed in the water, laughing
squealing, having some good time. At one point I saw
her "date" standing in the trees along the shore. I waved.
He turned and disappeared.

Later, when we walked back up the path, with our clothes
over our wet suits, they were waiting for us
where it opened out into a sunlit clearing.
They both looked grim, but I noticed that while
the smaller one's complexion was flushed, the bigger guy,
as he approached me, looked pale, looked gray.
Suddenly the light changed and everything
was moving in slow motion. I felt slightly nauseous,
and knew something was going to happen.

Without pausing, he reached me and swung.
His huge fist hit the left side of my jaw.
There was a flash of light, and I was down, hearing
my neighbor in the distance screaming, "No! No, don't!
Don't. I'm sorry. I'm sorry." He had done
what he had to do—no more, no less. By the time
I could again focus my eyes, and got up on an elbow,
his back was turned as he walked away. She was with
the smaller guy, talking quietly. I followed them
to where the older girl had a blanket spread
over the weeds. She was looking at a potato chip.

For the rest of the afternoon not a word
was said about what had happened. The big guy

seemed almost fatherly, and perhaps a little embarrassed.
My pal sat beside her date. I was across from them,
off the blanket, drinking beers. Several beers.

It was a lesson. I had inadvertently been caught
in a system of order that was both violent
and benign. I respected them, and felt they
had dealt with me as ethically as they could.

I did not belong there, and was, in a way,
both perpetrator and victim. I knew
if I ever again crossed paths with the guy
who had hit me, he'd consider me a friend.

Naming

Feeling the excitement
of discovery,

your surgeon gave
his own family names

to each of your organs.

Around the Bend

Where the stream widens
and offers a small beach,
there are two ducks—one of them
female.

When I fake the sound of ducks,
they both turn their heads
in my direction, then look away:

they've been visited by quacks before!

Then they both step into the water,
and the brightly colored one paddles
in circles around the other, as if to say:

"Let's get on with this!"
Then they're gone, upstream and
around the bend.

Lookout Creek

Sitting above Lookout Creek
on a knobby cliff, I notice
below me a perfectly round

cap on a mostly submerged boulder.
It looks like it could be the lid
on the deck of a submarine.

I would like to open this four-foot wide
door and descend into the forest
catacombs. But now

an amputee grasshopper climbs
my jeans and stops to look at me.
I believe he is saying I should not

waste my ability to think
on that wet rock. The moss is
enough. You are blessed.

Then he leaps at an angle off.

The Salamander

This Northwest forest is all about water,
and the beautiful reddish-brown Ensatina salamander
I met this morning is proof. I watched him
(or perhaps her) waddle across the wet ground,
sprinkled with orange pine needles. She looked
like a cartoon salamander, with her tender,
protruding eyes and delicate rib-like folds. I watched her
swim gracefully under a two-inch deep puddle.
When she emerged, and paused at the edge,
I carefully gathered her up, then made a cave
from my hand. With her sweet head peeking out,
she seemed to relax when I gently blew warm breath
on her. It was as though she was thinking: "Huh.
This isn't so bad. Nice bed." When I placed her back
in the puddle to enjoy watching her swim again,
she just floated there, limbs splayed out. For a few moments
I looked up into the trees, enjoying the mist cloaking them.
When I returned my gaze to find my salamander, he had
completely disappeared. So well-camouflaged in his color
and shape—no matter how carefully I scanned the puddle
and dirt around it, he was gone. And, of course, he had
to have been within a foot or two of where I'd put him down.
I wondered, how could a man become that invisible?

Pondering

Looking with pleasure up a mountain stream,
then following the path of water down
through channels in the rocky stream-bed,
I notice the flat area of a rock slab has a bowl
cut into it, where the water seems to slow and
swirl, as though it is taking time to consider
its own flow, where it has been, and what
it remembers. When that eddy rejoins the rush,
it seems brighter, with heightened
flecks of white.

Winter Spiders

Along the creek the sickly winter spiders
have finally begun to gather
under pieces of bark and rusted tin

Just in time for what little love they have
to join them like the earth
beneath the oceans
joins the distant island

Like a million whales all singing the same song

Winter Sapling

At a distance of one
hundred feet, we saw
a sapling with an encrustation

of ice and snow. Closer, where the bark
had split away—in an area at eye-level and
above—the moisture fanned out

into a long frill of lacey crystals, as though
the soul had needed to leave, but was frozen
in an oddly familiar gesture, temperature

too low perhaps for death
to complete its arduous project.

Then the sun came on,
and what had been spirit
began to run.

Ode to No Snow

Strolling past the cathedral bush,
long since the DVDs and CDs have hushed,
we approach the dim region of discord
where the neighborhood possum is Lord.

There are no brutal edges here
where only twigs, leaves and insects appear.
The comely chafers give their shine
while a half-moon drives the midges blind.

A rusting cleaver in a halo of wire
dims brown the flash of stars.
We'll find a long-tailed cat
to wear home like a coon-skin hat.

Winter Nocturne

1.
Through the trap door we let fall
what troubles us, then pull it shut.
All night we hear a weeping child
in the crawlspace. You say, "Let's
check it out in the morning."
I roll toward the wall and grunt
affirmation.

2.
We lay there, together, coming apart.
You feel things on your skin.
I see colors: red or blue or yellow—
each one shifts to a sick green.
We both hear the snap, of a finger or twig.
Then the heat begins.

3.
In the middle of the night there's muttering—
the refrigerator sounds like men
debating how best to torture us.
When the sound quits, we know
they're getting near.

Saved by Moss

It seems right—
here on my angled perch
atop the rocks above
Lookout Creek—
to feel I'm on the verge
of slipping off and
tumbling 30 feet
into the rushing water.
Only a half-inch thick
carpet of moss
saves me.

Toothpicks

All along Lookout Creek
there are enormous
old growth Douglas fir
that have become uprooted
and fallen into and over
the water. I call them Toothpicks
of the Forest God.

White Boulders

The round and whitened boulders
are bordered by light green foliage
below the massive, heavily shadowed
rock outcrop that supports a stand of trees
that reach toward the mountain ridge above.

This isn't the setting for some drama
or idea, this is the exquisite world we rise
and fall in. And below it all is
moving water that finds, and sweetens,
and carries life.

Endless

Gazing down this deep, rock-studded gorge
is like looking back over the 78 years of my life:

there are immense boulders in the path
of Mona Creek, but the life-bearing water always

finds its way. In the distance there are swaths
of dazzling green beside dense, hard-edged shadows.

At the farthest reach of vision, rising out of
the morning mist, is a mountain cloaked in trees.

Above that, endless blue.

About the Author

James Bertolino's poetry has received recognition through a Book-of-the-Month Club Poetry Fellowship, the Discovery Award, a National Endowment for the Arts fellowship, the 1996 International Merit Award in Poetry from *Atlanta Review*, two *Quarterly Review of Literature* book publication awards, and the Jeanne Lohmann Poetry Prize for Washington State Poets.

His poem "A Wedding Toast" appeared in 143 American newspapers several years ago, thanks to the "American Life in Poetry" column edited by former U.S. Poet Laureate Ted Kooser. He has had 12 volumes of poetry published, as well as numerous chapbooks. Recent collections include *Every Wound Has A Rhythm*, 2012, published by World Enough Writers, and *Ravenous Bliss: New and Selected Love Poems*, 2014, from MoonPath Press, and *Galaxy in Thrall*, 2019, from Goldfish Press. His most recent volume is the anthology he edited titled *Last Call*, where all the poems from poets in 31 states and four countries refer in some way to alcohol. It was published in 2018 by World Enough Writers in Tillamook, Oregon.

He received his Bachelor's degree from the University of Wisconsin-Oshkosh, and his MFA from Cornell University. Since 1965, he has had his poetry reprinted in 48 anthologies. He taught creative writing for 36 years at Cornell University, University of Cincinnati, Western Washington University and, in 2006, retired from a position as Poet-in-Residence at Willamette University in Oregon. He and Anita Boyle live on five acres near Bellingham, Washington.